Lynn Huggins-Cooper

Contents

Introduction

Children between the ages of 7 and 11 (Years 3–6) study Key Stage 2 of the National Curriculum. In May of their final year in Key Stage 2 (Year 6) all children take written national Tests (commonly known as SATs) in English, Mathematics and Science. The tests are carried out in school, under the supervision of teachers, but are marked by examiners outside the school.

Pupils also have their school work assessed by their teachers. These assessments will be set alongside your child's results in the National Tests. In July these results will be reported to you, enabling you and your child's teacher to see whether your child is reaching national standards set out in the National Curriculum. The report will highlight your child's strengths and achievements and will suggest targets for development. Each child will probably spend about five hours in total sitting the tests during one week in May. Most children will do two papers in Science and three papers in Mathematics and English.

**Understanding your child's
level of achievement**

The National Curriculum divides standards of performance in each subject into a number of levels, from 1 to 8. On average, children are expected to advance one level for every two years they are at school. By the end of Key Stage 2 (Year 6), the majority of children will have reached level 4.

The table shows how your child should progress through the levels at ages 7, 11 and 14 (the end of Key Stage 3).

	7 years	11 years	14 years
level 8+			☐
level 8			■
level 7			■
level 6		☐	☐
level 5		■	☐
level 4	☐	☐	■
level 3	■	■	■
level 2	☐	■	■
level 1	■	■	■

☐ Exceptional performance

■ Exceeded targets for age group

☐ Achieved targets for age group

■ Working towards targets for age group

The Tests in English

The National Curriculum divides English into three areas or Attainment Targets. These are 'Speaking and Listening', which is assessed through classroom work, and 'Reading' and 'Writing' for which there are written tests. There is also a short written test for 'Spelling and Handwriting'.

Reading test (1 hour)
This tests your child's understanding of a reading passage, and requires evidence to be shown from it to support answers.

Writing test (1 hour)
This tests your child's ability to organise and present the content of a piece of writing, and to spell and punctuate correctly.

Spelling and Handwriting test (15 minutes)
This tests your child's ability to spell words in the context of a passage read aloud, and to write out neatly a short piece of printed text.

Levels of attainment

Most children will take the tests for Levels 3–5, and this book is designed to assist children working at these levels. The exercises cover all the areas your child will meet in Key Stage 2 English, and working through them will help to consolidate skills and identify those which need further practice to achieve Level 4.

Children achieving Level 5 use a variety of vocabulary, and are aware of different styles of writing and the level of formality they require. Level 5 work is well presented; the handwriting style is mature and legible, and spelling and grammatical conventions are usually correct.

Children who consistently achieve Level 5 standard during Year 6 may be entered for the Level 6 Extension Paper. This book does not attempt to revise work to this level, but notes are given on page 47 explaining the criteria which are applied in assessing Level 6 work, with brief advice on extending a child's skills in English.

How this book will help

- This book provides the essential knowledge needed by your child to tackle the English tests with confidence.
- It revises work your child should be doing in class. It does not attempt to teach new material from scratch.
- It is designed to help your child prepare for the tests. It includes activities to help your child reflect on reading matter and improve comprehension skills, to develop writing abilities and to improve spelling and handwriting.
- Useful 'tips' help your child to develop work further.
- Examples of 'good' answers give your child a model to work from.
- Tests (Test yourself pages) allow your child informal practice in answering the kinds of questions asked in the National Tests. If your child finds the tests, (or a part of one) hard, the topics covered in that section of the book should be revised again.
- Answers are provided at the back of the book to enable your child to learn from mistakes.

Using this book

Short questions can be answered on the page, but have some spare paper available for your child to use when working on longer activities. In encouraging your child, remember the 'little and often' rule. Make sure the atmosphere is relaxed when this book is used. It can be returned to again and again, but try to make sure your child does not spend too much time worrying, and encourage a relaxed and confident approach. Help your child to see the SATs tests as an opportunity to demonstrate knowledge rather than worrying about any difficulties. This book has been designed to provide a fun way of practising the skills and knowledge necessary for your child to produce the best possible work in the National Tests.

1 Word gems

You should be able to describe the words used in a story or passage, saying how they create a mood or feeling. Read the passage below and the comments afterwards.

> The mist rose in tendrils, like icy wraiths swirling and dancing sinuously upwards from the hollow dips that studded the field. The dripping hawthorn hedge, festooned with droplets of condensed water, was the only thing that broke the silence. Charlotte swung her legs *aimlessly* as she sat on the gate, *gazing at but not seeing* the unearthly beauty unfolding before her. She *watched without interest* as the water dripped onto her trainers, spreading to make a dark stain like a chromatogram. She was twelve years old.
>
> From *A Time of Change* by Lynn Huggins-Cooper

The words in blue set the mood; they make you feel as though something strange or mysterious is about to happen. The words in *italics* tell you about Charlotte's mood: she is bored. These words or phrases paint a picture of the story in our 'mind's eye'.

You could choose these words as 'word gems':
tendrils, icy wraiths, swirling
These sound wet and slithery, and a little strange because of the repeated 's' sounds they contain (see 'alliteration' on page 5). There are many more words in the passage that help create the mood and set the scene.

Activity

List all the other words in the passage that you would choose as 'word gems'. Say why you have chosen them.

Tip

In your SATs test, as long as you can say why certain words or phrases help create a mood or feeling, there are no 'right' or 'wrong' answers.

2 Word magic

When you are writing stories, always use exciting language. In your SATs, interesting and varied vocabulary will help you to get extra marks!

You could try:

Onomatopoeia: when a word sounds like the thing it is describing.

These words are all onomatopoeic.

Alliteration: words used together that have the same initial sound.

- whispering wind
- slimy slugs
- smelly smog
- lazy lions
- noisy neighbours
- wiggly worms
- sizzling sausages
- glistening gold
- slithering snakes

Question

Fill the gaps with alliterative adjectives (describing words):

The _____ frog jumped into the _____ water and swam past a _____ goldfish hiding among the rocks.

Activity

Look through a chapter or a section of a book you have read. List all the onomatopoeic words you can find. Start your own collection of onomatopoeic words to use in your stories.

Tip

Collect words and phrases from the books that you read. Keep them in a notebook.

3 How does it feel?

When you answer questions on a passage you have read, you should comment on the feelings of the characters involved. It is more interesting if you use 'shades of feeling' rather than basic words such as 'happy', 'sad' or 'cross'.

This is part of a page from a thesaurus.

disentangle

disentangle verb
1 to disentangle hair.
sort out, straighten out, unknot, untangle
2 The cat disentangled itself from the brambles.
free, liberate, release
disfigure verb
She was disfigured by a scar.
damage, deform, make ugly, spoil
disgrace noun
was upset at the ...ing last in

dishonour

horrible, nauseating, repulsive, revolting
dish noun
1 She ate from a silver dish.
bowl, plate
2 Banana split is my favourite dish.
food, item on the menu
dishearten verb
The torrential rain disheartened the campers.
depress. dismay, put off, sadden
dishevelled adjective
dishevelled appearance.
...aggled, messy, scruffy, ...tidy ...ishonest

Here is a list of 'feelings' words. Look in a thesaurus for extra words.

anxious – worried

sceptical – not ready to believe; suspicious

intrigued – very interested; wanting to know more

relieved – feeling better, more relaxed about something you have been nervous about

curious – keen to find out about things

satisfied – content

angry – cross

confused – not understanding; puzzled

disappointed – feeling let down about something

Question

What do these 'feelings' words mean?

depressed

distraught

ecstatic

Activity

Make a list of your own 'feelings' words and their meanings.

Tip

Collect 'feelings' words from books, magazines, newspapers, television and radio. (People are often asked about their feelings during an interview.)

4 School report

In the SATs reading test you will be asked to comment on characters. Read this report on Jack, from *Jack and the Beanstalk*.

Name Jack Beanstalk

English

Jack's English would improve generally if he listened more carefully to instructions.

Mathematics

Jack must try harder. His grasp of the value of money is very limited indeed.

Science

Jack has shown great interest in our project on plant life and growth. His 'bean growing' experiment was quite outstanding!

PE

Jack is an athletic boy, excelling at the 'climbing' option.

General Comments

I am sure that with a little extra concentration Jack will make some giant leaps forward in the near future.

Question

Choose three words of your own to describe Jack.

Activity

Write a 'school report' on a character from a book you have read recently. Your comments need to reflect the content of the story and what you have found out about the character.

Tip

As you read, think about the personality of the characters and why they act the way they do.

5 The crime scene

The way a character behaves tells you what sort of person they are. Look at the scene at the Three Bears' cottage, then read about the suspect.

Alpha Bravo 3, come in, please ...can you report your findings?

Alpha Bravo 3 reporting, sergeant ... scene as reported by householder Mrs. Bear ... chairs overturned and broken ... quantity of oatmeal type commodity stolen. We have a description of the suspect as she left the scene – blonde, female, about 4ft tall. I also have a likely character profile of the suspect given to us by the forensic psychologist.

Character profile of suspect

Impetuous: an 'opportunist' crime; the door was unlocked so she entered on the spur of the moment. The crime bears no sign of premeditation.

Selfish: helped herself to breakfast clearly laid out for a family.

Sense of novelty or inability to make decisions: had tried each chair 'for size'; had sampled each bowl of porridge.

Careless: left a trail of oatmeal up to the bedroom; didn't try to cover tracks – left beds rumpled.

Question

Write down two new words to describe the suspect.

Activity

Choose a book you have read and write a character profile. What is the character like; how do you know, and where is your 'evidence'?

Tip

Remember, in commenting on your chosen character you should refer back to the text for 'evidence.'

6 Reading recipe

Read Maria's 'book recipe': all the good things in a book she has enjoyed.

Recipe for: 'Pongwiffy' by Kaye Umansky

Ingredients: rich, well-rounded, full flavoured characters. You feel as if you know them. Give examples.

Pongwiffy has terrible manners. She says to her friend Sharkadder, 'What on earth do you need a spoon for? Slurp it from the plate like I'm doing.' (page 11). Hugo is a fierce hamster, and Pongwiffy's familiar. His favourite saying is 'Vant a fight?'

Blend well with: an exciting plot with interesting undercurrents. What does it boil down to?

Awful goblins move in next door to Pongwiffy. She moves in with her friend Sharkadder who helps her to find a new 'hovel' and a 'familiar' who turns out to be a fierce hamster! There is a talent contest for the witches, and exciting things start to happen.

Mix with: speech, dialogue. Does the author use what the characters say to develop the plot? Give examples.

The author uses Sharkadder to describe Pongwiffy's cave. 'It's a smelly little slum. It's not fit to live in. It's sordid and yucky. It suits you.' (page 9).

Season with: tangy, thrilling descriptions.

'Thick black steam belched from horrible looking slop which bubbled and glopped in the cauldron.' (page 8). 'Squiggly strands of greasy hair hung like potato peelings down her back.' (page 59).

Garnish and serve with: fresh, crisp language washed down with a sparkling glass of refreshing words such as:

congealed, repulsive, stale spiderspread sandwiches, stinkpot.

Activity

Choose a book you know and write a recipe for it.

Tip

As you read, think about the ingredients that go into a good story, and how the author has included them.

9

7 Desert island characters

You are drifting on a raft on a vast, glittering ocean. Suddenly you spot land on the horizon. As you get closer, you can see someone waving. It is a character from your favourite book! Who would you like it to be?

Read about Sammy's choice and his answers to the questions.

Comment on the type of person you have chosen. Explain your choice.

> I would choose Stig from 'Stig of the Dump' by Clive King. He can make all sorts of useful things out of junk that he finds, so if we found anything useful on the drift line like wood or rubbish washed up by the sea he would be able to make things to make our lives more comfortable.

Would they be useful because of special skills or knowledge? Would they be interesting to be with?

> Stig can make arrowheads out of flints, and hunts for food, so he would help to feed us. He made a comfortable home in a cave, and he knows how to chop wood to make fires. This would make him a useful companion, as he would be able to keep us warm and sheltered.
>
> Stig is good at problem solving. On page 156, it says 'Whenever there was a particularly odd job to be done (like making sure a rainwater butt didn't spring a leak when it was empty and overflow when it was full — or inventing a new tool for lifting parsnips) then someone would say "Let's get Stig to fix it!"
>
> Stig is artistic and draws imaginative pictures on the walls of his cave, telling the stories of hunts he has been on. This would make him an interesting companion because he could teach me how to draw like him.

Activity

Write down the name of the character you would choose to have with you on a desert island, and the reasons for your choice.

Tip

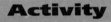

Keep a 'character log'. As you read a book, jot down a few notes about the characters and the reasons for their actions.

8 Whose story?

The letters below recount the same events in *The Tempest* by William Shakespeare – but from very different points of view!

From Caliban, the beast, to his mother:

makes seaweed sound lovely – even tasty!

he thinks Miranda is beautiful

Dearest Mother,
The morning after a terrible storm, I found an angel lying on the beach amongst the succulent seaweed. I thought I would be able to keep her, but her father, Prospero, came and would not let me. I went to live with them in a dark cave. One night I tried to steal a tiny kiss from Miranda. There was such a hue and cry! Now I am banished from the cave!

thought he was being gentle

Your loving son,
Caliban.

From Miranda, the heroine, to her lady in waiting:

she is scared of Caliban and thinks he is ugly

finds the island unpleasant

My dearest,
I awoke, shipwrecked on a beach covered in smelly seaweed. A terrible beast with staring eyes, scaly skin and drooling lips was towering over me – ugh! Fortunately Father appeared to save me, but then he asked the beast to lodge with us! To top it all, last night, the ghastly creature slobbered on me whilst I was sleeping! At least now Father has sent him away. Please write soon!

finds his behaviour revolting

Miranda.

Activity

Choose a book you have been reading, and write letters from two characters writing about the same event from different points of view.

Tip

Try to think of the 'two sides to every story' as you read your own books.

9 Between the lines

Sometimes authors give a message through their writing. Read what Asif wrote about *Flour Babies* by Anne Fine.

What was the author's 'hidden message'?

The A class is working on a science project for the school fair. The message of the book is about the responsibilities of being a parent. Some of the class seemed to 'grow up' through the project, which made them think about caring. Simon is described as a 'committed hooligan' at the beginning of the book, but by the end, his teacher, Mr. Cartright, tells him, 'If keeping what you care for close and safe counts for anything, I'll tell you this. You'll make a better father than most.' (page 136).

Does the story (or any others you have read by the same author) give us any clues about the author, or what they care about?

The author seems interested in the way people feel, and the way this affects their actions. Anne Fine seems to know how teenagers feel. She wrote about a girl's relationship with her stepfather in 'Goggle Eyes'. Perhaps she listens hard to young people or maybe she remembers clearly what it feels like to be a teenager.

Did the story make you think about yourself and the way you act or have acted in the past?

The book makes you think about your parents and the time they have spent caring for you, which I had not thought about much. Simon thinks about his dad, who left when he was a baby, and the way he feels about the project helps him to understand why. It makes you think that it is hard work to be a parent, but as Simon starts to care about his flour baby you think that there are good things about being a parent, too.

Activity

Choose a book from the list below, or one of your own, and use the questions to write about the author's message.

Freaky Friday
Mary Rodgers

Piggybook
Anthony Browne

Dinosaurs and All That Rubbish
Michael Foreman

The Iron Woman
Ted Hughes

Tip

If you read 'between the lines' to answer questions in your SATs, always refer to evidence in the actual piece of writing to support your view.

12

10 Predict the future!

Read Beth's answers to these questions about the first chapter of *The Iron Man* by Ted Hughes.

Does the first chapter excite you, making you want to read more? Can you say why or why not?

Yes, because the chapter starts with lots of questions 'Where had he come from? Nobody knows.' He falls from a cliff and smashes, then the pieces start to find each other, and put the Iron Man back together.

Who are the main characters, in your opinion? Why?

Chapter one only talks about the Iron Man, so you feel that he is going to be the most important character.

What are they like? Do you think you would be friends if you met? Why?

The Iron Man is mysterious. We don't know much about him, except that he is patient and spends a long time looking for his body parts to put them back together. You would have to know him better before you knew if you wanted to be his friend.

What do you think will happen next in the story? Is there anything in the first chapter that gives you a clue?

You feel as though the Iron Man is going somewhere. He seems to have a purpose as he walks out to sea 'deeper, deeper, deeper' (page 17). Perhaps he will have adventures underwater, or get to a beach somewhere.

Is there a main problem in the story, or something the main character will have to solve or accept? How do you think they will do this?

You don't know this from the first chapter. The Iron Man has a problem in chapter one because he smashes and has to be put back together again.

Now read on.

Now you have finished the book!

Were your predictions right? Did you find clues in the first chapter for what happened later?

He was going somewhere — to find scrap metal, to eat. He saves the world from a Space Dragon, which you could not work out from the first chapter — but you did know that the Iron Man was extraordinary!

Activity

Read the first chapter of a book. STOP! Predict what happens next. Use the questions.

Tip

Prediction helps you to develop your understanding of what you are reading.

11 Be a detective!

You are Chief Inspector Boggis of the 'Good Books' Unit, tracking down good books. You need to take case notes on all the books you read. Look at the questions David answered after reading *The Lion, the Witch and the Wardrobe* by C.S. Lewis.

Characters: Who are the main characters? Who are the villains? Are there any heroes or heroines?

Lucy, Edmund, Susan, Peter — brothers and sisters.
Mr Tumnus — faun
Aslan — hero; a lion
White Witch — evil villainess
Mr and Mrs Beaver

Key incident: What happens, to whom and why?

Children go to a secret world called Narnia through a wardrobe. Edmund goes with the Witch to her palace. She has created never ending winter. The other children try to help Aslan to free Narnia — but to save Edmund, Aslan sacrifices himself and dies. Powerful magic brings Aslan back to life, and he kills the witch. The children rule Narnia now it is free.

Location: Where does the main action take place? Does this affect the outcome?

Narnia — a place where magic can and does happen, and animals talk and act as people do in the real world. Many strange creatures who are important to the story only exist in Narnia, not the real world, such as Mr Tumnus the faun, and the witch's evil army — giants and monsters.

Motives: Why do the characters act and react as they do? Does anything excuse their actions? Give evidence.

Edmund seems very selfish. He pretends Narnia is not real, so Susan and Peter think Lucy is making it up. He goes off with the White Witch, so we could think he is evil too — but he has eaten enchanted turkish delight and we find out that anyone who tastes it craves more and will do anything to get it. On page 83, it says people who have eaten the turkish delight 'would even, if they were allowed, go on eating it till they killed themselves.' So when Edmund runs away to the witch to tell her where his brother and sisters are, he perhaps has an excuse.

Later in the book, Edmund is healed by Lucy's magic cordial and his sister says he looks better than he has since 'his first term at that horrid school which was where he had begun to go wrong' (page 163). He may have been changed by the way he was treated at school.

Mr Tumnus takes Lucy to his home and plans to give her to the Witch. This seems awful and treacherous, but he does it because he is afraid. On page 24 he says 'She'll have my tail cut off, and my horns sawn off, and my beard plucked out, and she'll wave her hands over my beautiful cloven hooves and turn them into horrid solid hooves like a wretched horse's.' Later on he tries to help the children and does not seem to be a bad creature.

Result of investigation: What happened in the end? Is it a 'fair' ending?

Good wins and evil is beaten. The Witch is killed and Aslan is alive again. The children rule as Kings and Queens and Narnia is safe. Eventually, they go back through the wardrobe to the real world.

Would you recommend this book, and why?

I would recommend this book because it is exciting and full of imaginative ideas, events and characters. The descriptions are excellent.

Activity

Use the questions to write about a book you have enjoyed.

Characters
Key Incidents
Location
Motives
Result of Investigation

Tip

Always include 'evidence' in your answers. Using quotations from the passage will help to 'prove' your case!

12 Questions, questions!

Alex is reviewing *The Hobbit* by J.R.R. Tolkein.

How would you feel by the end of the book if you were the main character?

I would feel different. I would have changed because of my experiences. By the end of 'The Hobbit', Bilbo Baggins, the main character, has developed into an outstanding and unusual Hobbit. If I were him, I would feel proud and special.

Have you ever felt like any of the characters in this book in real life? If so, when and why?

I have felt like one of the dwarves — knowing that there must be more to life, and that something is out there, waiting for you to take it and make it your own.

With which character did you identify most closely. Why?

I identified most with the Wood Elf King. He is concerned about the environment, and the need to respect the natural world. I am a keen conservationist. The Wood Elf King loves huge, noisy parties. So do I!

Do you know anyone in real life like the characters in this book? How are they similar?

I have friends that share some of Bilbo Baggins' characteristics. They can be shy, and back away from adventure like Bilbo, who just wants to be an ordinary Hobbit until he is forced into action by events in the story.

Have you read any books similar to this one?

The 'Redwall' books by Brian Jaques are similar even though the characters are animals. I think the author may have been influenced by Tolkein stories such as 'The Hobbit.'

Did you guess the ending before it happened? If so, were you right? What gave you clues about the ending?

I would never have guessed the ending! Unexpected things kept happening to throw my predictions off course. That is one of the reasons I enjoyed the book so much.

Who would you recommend this story to and why?

I would strongly recommend this book to anyone who likes fantasy writing. If, like me, you are keen on fantasy wargaming you will find this book inspirational!

Activity

Choose a story you have read recently, and use the questions to help you to review the book.

Tip

When questions ask for your opinion, you must refer to the text to show your understanding of what you have read.

Reading fiction and non-fiction

Fiction and non-fiction sometimes need different styles of reading. You will read both fiction and non-fiction in the SATs test. Study the checklist below to compare the two styles.

Fiction (stories)

1 Fast, fluent reading to find out 'what happens next.'

2 Fiction is read from beginning to end in sequence.

3 The meaning of new vocabulary can often be worked out from the setting and context.

4 Fiction is not usually illustrated for older readers – the author relies entirely on the words to tell the story.

5. The author's style is often personal.

Non-fiction (information)

1 Skimming and scanning are necessary to extract information (see page 20) followed by slower, careful reading to absorb facts.

2 Non-fiction is often read to extract information, 'dipping in', rather than reading straight through.

3 Specialised vocabulary often requires a glossary to explain words.

4 Non-fiction is usually illustrated. Photographs, diagrams, charts or graphs help to explain the subject matter of the book.

5 The author's style is usually impersonal. The text is about 'hard facts' rather than feelings.

Question

Name one fiction and one non-fiction book you have read.

Activity

Look at a selection of fiction and non-fiction books. Try to identify differences described in the lists, and any other differences between fiction and non-fiction.

Tip

When you read a story about a specific subject, compare it with a non-fiction book covering the same subject.

Unanswered questions

Do you know how to get information from books?

Michael chose to find out about a topic that interested him. He wrote some questions and then set off to find the answers from books in school and at the local library.

Before he started, he

- made his choice of subject quite narrow – 'The Crab' instead of a broad subject like 'Seashore Life'.

- made sure he knew how to use a contents page, an index and a glossary.

Read the questions Michael wrote for his topic.

What happens when crabs grow?

What are the crab's predators?

What do crabs eat?

Where do crabs live?

What do crab babies look like?

15 Comprehension skills

Comprehension tests your understanding of what you have read. In the SATs tests, the questions can seem quite complicated. Any answer should refer back to the text for evidence, so the more practice you have, the better!

Read the passage below, and the suggested answers to the questions.

Question

In the passage about the storm, what does the writer think was the most frightening aspect of the damage?

Last night there was a terrible storm which created havoc for the emergency services throughout the country. The South of England, which bore the brunt of the winds, has never experienced anything so devastating. Majestic oak trees planted during the reign of Henry VIII were torn down by the high winds. The landscape of Sussex has been changed forever, as gaping wounds have appeared in parks and woodland. Perhaps the greatest damage, however, has been to our sense of security as we realise that for all the benefits of modern technology, we are still at Nature's mercy.

1. **Which part of the country suffered most damage?**
   The South of England 'bore the brunt' of the wind. This means it was hit by the strongest winds. The passage also tells us that Sussex suffered terrible damage, and Sussex is in the South of England.

2. **Were the trees that were uprooted old? How do you know?**
   The trees that were blown down were very old. We know this because the passage says that trees, '… planted in the reign of Henry VIII were torn down by high winds.'

Tip

You can quote from the text to support your opinion.

16 Skimming and scanning

These skills help you to extract information in order to answer comprehension questions – so they are very useful for SATs tests!

Skimming: you read through a passage quickly to establish what it is about.

Scanning: you sweep the page with your eyes to find the answers to specific questions. You look for **key words** or **key phrases** to locate parts of the text to read through slowly in order to extract the facts you need.

Tip

Always read a comprehension passage through several times before you start to tackle the questions.

Read the passage below.

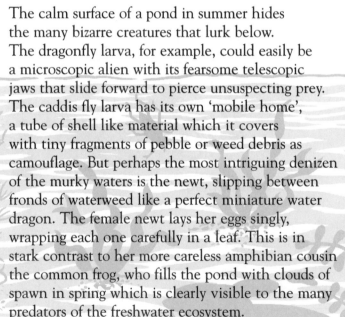

The calm surface of a pond in summer hides the many bizarre creatures that lurk below. The dragonfly larva, for example, could easily be a microscopic alien with its fearsome telescopic jaws that slide forward to pierce unsuspecting prey. The caddis fly larva has its own 'mobile home', a tube of shell like material which it covers with tiny fragments of pebble or weed debris as camouflage. But perhaps the most intriguing denizen of the murky waters is the newt, slipping between fronds of waterweed like a perfect miniature water dragon. The female newt lays her eggs singly, wrapping each one carefully in a leaf. This is in stark contrast to her more careless amphibian cousin the common frog, who fills the pond with clouds of spawn in spring which is clearly visible to the many predators of the freshwater ecosystem.

Now read the questions and the 'Strategies for answering' on the next page.

Question A: How does the newt's egg-laying technique differ from that of the common frog?

Strategies for answering:

1 Before attempting any questions, skim read the article to see what it is about.
2 Scan the text to find the relevant piece of the passage. Scan for these key words from the question: egg, newt, frog.
3 Having found the key words, read that part of the passage slowly in order to extract the information needed to answer the question.

Answer: **The newt lays its eggs one at a time, wrapping each one in a leaf. The frog lays lots of spawn and abandons it.**

Question B: What is unusual about the caddis fly larva's home?

Strategies for answering:

Having already skimmed the article, go straight to scanning.
1 Scan for the relevant part of the article, using these key words from the question: caddis fly larva, home.
2 Having found the key words, read the relevant part of the passage slowly in order to extract the information needed to answer the question.

Answer: **The caddis fly larva's home is portable; it moves around with the larva. It is cleverly camouflaged with bits of stone and weed found on the bottom of the pond.**

Question C: How does the dragonfly larva kill its prey?

Strategies for answering:

Having already skimmed the article, go straight to scanning.
1 Scan for the relevant part of the article, using these key words from the question: dragonfly larva, prey.
2 Having found the key words, read that part of the passage slowly in order to extract the information needed to answer the question.

Answer: **The dragonfly larva kills its prey with its telescopic jaw.**

Question

What creature does the writer say the newt is like?

Activity

Choose a passage from a non-fiction book. Skim it. Ask yourself a question, then scan the passage to see if you can find the answer quickly.

17 Test 1

Read this passage about rockpools, and then answer the
questions. If you have read the passage through several
times, and have a good grasp of what it is about, you will
be able to scan it quickly when you are looking for answers.

Tip

Don't forget to
skim the passage
through several
times before you
attempt the questions.

Rockpools are fabulous natural aquaria, full of creatures
stranded by the tide each day. They give us an exciting
opportunity to glimpse sea creatures as they act in their
natural habitat. Take the beadlet anemone, for example.
Stuck fast to the rocks, the red or green beadlet anemone
looks like a blob of jelly when the tide is out. But in the
world of the rockpool we see a different creature. Submerged
in water, the anemone stretches out its tentacles to wave like
hair. As an unsuspecting shrimp or fish touches the tentacles,
thousands of tiny harpoon type stings shoot out, pinning the
prey and injecting it with lethal venom. Looking between
the rocks, one may be fortunate enough to see a fish hidden
in the weed, such as the red gurnard or 'walking fish' as it is
sometimes known as a result of the leg-like probes with
which it searches for food.

Perhaps the most fascinating denizen of the rockpool is the
hermit crab. Unlike the shore crab, this soft bodied crab does
not have a shell of its own, and in order to hide from
predators it inhabits the discarded shells of the snail-like
creatures that live on rocky shorelines. A tiny hermit crab
may live in the shell of a periwinkle or necklace shell, but as
it grows it has to find a bigger home to move into. This is a
risky manoeuvre, with many marine predators eager to
gobble a morsel of soft bodied crab. In time, the hermit crab
will grow large enough to fill a whelk shell.

1 What happens when a creature brushes against the tentacles of the beadlet anemone?

Key words to scan for: _____

Answer: _____

_____

2 Why does the red gurnard also have the name 'walking fish'?

Key words to scan for: _____

Answer: _____

_____

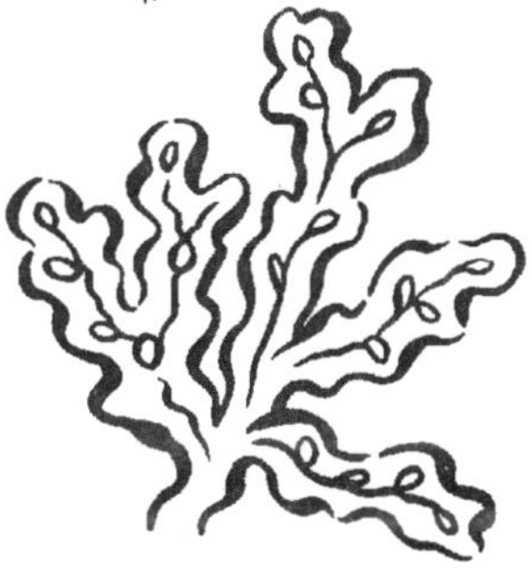

3 How does the hermit crab differ from the shore crab?

Key words to scan for: _____

Answer: _____

_____

4 Where might a tiny hermit crab choose to live?

Key words to scan for: _____

Answer: _____

_____

5 Why is moving from one shell to another dangerous for a hermit crab?

Key words to scan for: _____

Answer: _____

_____

18 Brainstorming

Before writers begin their work, they often 'brainstorm' their thoughts and make a note of useful words and phrases. Here is a brainstorm on the subject of the seashore for an article for the *Wildlife Watch Club* newsletter:

Pollution levels - factors

Responsible rockpooling - St. Mary's island rules

Report of clean up at Haven

Tide line "finds"
- mermaid's purse
- ray bones

Activity

Now it's your turn. Choose a topic for an article. Do you belong to a club, or have an interesting hobby? Write your brainstorm in the bubble. All you need to include are first thoughts, and useful words and phrases. You do not need to write in full sentences.

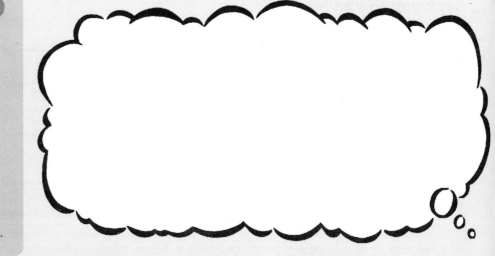

19 Collecting vocabulary

All writing is improved by exciting and varied use of vocabulary. This is the same whether you are writing a story or a piece of non-fiction. Using interesting vocabulary in your SATs can even gain marks!

On page 24 you read a brainstorm for an article on **The Seashore.** Here is a collection of descriptive vocabulary for that article:

- *glinting*
- *swirling water*
- *buffeting wind*
- *shimmering*

- *tang of salt on your lips*
- *scavenging crabs*
- *satisfying 'pop' of bladderwrack*
- *fronds of seaweed*

When you are collecting vocabulary, bear in mind:

unusual words that are new to you, and you may like to learn to use in the future.

words that sound interesting as you say them, like 'bladderwrack' in the article. You may wish to include onomatopoeic words (words that make a sound like the thing they describe) like 'pop', or alliterative words (words with repeated initial sounds) like 'whispering whales.' Read 'Word Magic' on page 5 for more details.

descriptive phrases (like 'tang of salt on your lips') that appeal to the senses of sight, smell, taste, hearing and touch.

Activity

You have written a brainstorm for an article. Now make a collection of interesting vocabulary to include in your writing.

Tip

Don't be afraid to 'borrow' words and phrases that you find when you are reading books, magazines and newspapers.

Build your own thesaurus!

A THESAURUS is a very useful book: it gives you lists of words with the same meaning so that you can make your writing interesting and varied.

You will come across interesting words by reading novels, poetry, plays, information books, magazines, newspapers and comics. You can even learn new vocabulary from the radio and television!

Not just SMELL but ...	Not just BIG but ...	Not just SAD but ...
reek	huge	unhappy
fragrance	massive	depressed
aroma	enormous	desolate
pungence	vast	tearful
odour	gigantic	upset
whiff	titanic	dejected
stink	large	gloomy
scent	gargantuan	miserable

Not just SHINY but ...	Not just SMALL but ...	Not just HAPPY but ...
glossy	tiny	joyful
glistening	miniscule	delighted
sparkling	miniature	glad
burnished	microscopic	cheerful
gleaming	diminutive	pleased
glimmering	petite	contented
glittering	minute	merry

Activity

Start to build your own thesaurus. Find as many different words as you can for:

bad

good

pretty

Tip

Make a list of all the new words you come across and find out what they mean.

The writing process

When you write a story, you go through several different stages:

Brainstorming	(first ideas)	(see page 24)
Planning	(organising ideas)	(see page 29)
First draft	(rough copy)	(see below)
Editing	(punctuation, spelling)	(see page 46)
Publishing	(final copy, handwriting)	(see page 44)

When you get to the 'first draft' or rough stage, use this checklist to help you improve your work.

Checklist

1 Does your story relate to the title you were given?
2 Is your story well structured; does it have a beginning, a middle and an end?
3 Does your story make sense?
4 Is the first paragraph interesting? Will it excite readers, and make them want to read more?
5 Does the story develop quickly?
6 Have you used descriptive words?
7 Is there a good strong ending or does the story just 'fizzle out'?

When you move on to the 'editing' stage, you should check your punctuation and spelling. The final stage is the 'publishing' of the story, by word processing or writing it out neatly and illustrating it.

For your writing test, you will be given 15 minutes to plan, and 45 minutes to write the whole piece. You will not have time to write a rough copy. You only have time to plan your ideas in note form. But still use the checklist to make sure you have included the right elements before you start to write.

Activity

Brainstorm ideas for a story. Write a first draft. Use the checklist to improve it.

Tip

Remember, your story will be marked for structure, style, use of varied vocabulary, and punctuation.

22 Story starters

The rustling sound grew cl...

The SATs test offers you a story option. You are usually given a title and have to write a story to fit. This becomes easier with practice!

Practise planning before you write. Read the story starters below. Shirin has written her ideas for the first story starter using the planner on the next page.

1   The rustling sound grew closer. I caught blurred movement in the corner of my eye. I turned, breathing harder, and there it was ...

2   The creature nuzzled gently at my outstretched hand. I could feel her warm breath as it hit my fingers before billowing away in a cloud of whiteness.

3   I watched the raindrop as it journeyed down the window pane, gathering speed. As it joined the pool on the sill, I stared off into the glowering sky. Soon I would be making a journey of my own.

4   I could feel the searing heat of the flames as I got closer. The horses were beating the walls of the stables with their hooves as they began to smell smoke. There was nobody else around – I'd have to lead them out myself!

Tip

Read a variety of books, including adventure stories, fables, traditional tales from different cultures, mysteries, plays, historical stories, myths and legends.

Activity

Choose one of the story starters and use the planner on page 29 to organise your ideas. Write the story.

23 Story planner

This is Shirin's plan for the first starter.

Where does your story begin? Can you describe the place?

In the swamp — dark, damp, eerie. Lots of strange noises, animals calling to each other in the dark. Trees growing close together, twisted, hideous trunks and branches like monster hands. Ground slurps as you walk

Who is going to appear in your story?

Mysterious, weeping boy who keeps disappearing. Parents who do not believe the boy really exists. Group of friends: Jagdep, Tom, Charlotte and David — investigate strange lights and noises coming from the swamp.

What is the exciting beginning to set the scene and 'hook' the reader?

The rustling sound grew closer. I caught blurred movement in the corner of my eye. I turned, breathing harder, and there it was — a small, white hand parting the branches. Someone was watching me! I stumbled forwards.

What happens during the story?

Boy is part of a group of travelling people who do not realise that the war that ended 120 years ago is over — they believe the only safe place is their camp in the middle of the swamp. The boy befriends the children and they learn about his old fashioned lifestyle — they show him modern things like digital watches. The children have to decide whether to keep their new friends a secret or not.

What is the good strong ending?

As the children walked slowly away, they heard a bird start to sing, first one, then a whole flock. "I know we made the right decision," said Jagdep as the birds rose in a cloud to wheel away towards the freedom of the open sky.

To get your own story started, answer the questions above.

Tip

Make sure your story has a beginning for 'scene setting', a middle 'action section', and a good strong ending.

24 Character profiling

Do the characters in the stories you write seem 'real'? Can you create characters so that readers feel they know them? When you discuss characters in the books you have read, can you describe their 'character profile'?

The character profile below is for the character of 'the boy' in the story plan on page 29.

Character Profile

Name Ezekial Moore

Appearance
small, pale skin, very dark brown eyes. Clothes are old fashioned style, handspun rough material.

Voice
speaks softly at first as though afraid of being overheard, but voice becomes louder and more confident as he gets to know the children. Uses old fashioned words, doesn't understand slang like O.K. etc.

Walk
moves with light steps — teases other children for being clumsy. Runs quickly, dodging in and out of trees and boggy patches. At first the children think he is a ghost because of his light-footed walk; he barely disturbs the undergrowth as he moves.

What sort of person is the character?
wary at first, suspicious of the children. As becomes more relaxed, boy is cheerful, intelligent and ready with quick solutions to problems. Likes jokes and spinning stories.

Activity

Think of a character for one of the story starters on page 28. Use the headings on this page to write a short description of him or her — or it!

Tip

As you read books, think about the language the author has used to make a vivid picture of the characters.

Planning non-fictional writing

Your SATs writing test will give you a choice between story writing and non-fictional writing such as a letter or a piece of 'information' writing.

There will be a planning sheet in the booklet for information writing. This will give you 'prompts' to help you to decide what to include, and the structure your writing should take. You will have 15 minutes to plan, the same as for a story.

Read Anna's plan for a piece of personal writing.

Early Memories

Set the scene. What did you look like?
curly hair, chubby, scowling on photos!

Pre-school memories
fingers caught in car door — sister Tina crying. Getting kittens Lady and Tramp — Tramp eating Christmas decorations.

'Starting school' memories
shiny shoes, purse on a strap, green knickers with pockets! Making a 'secret garden.' Meeting best friends Jackie and Tatiana.

Favourite games/toys
Orinoco Womble, French skipping, 'power balls'.

How does remembering make you feel?
A mixture of happy and sad memories — memories are important; they stay with us forever. Can we make 'good' memories for others?

Activity

Make notes using the questions and headings on the plan. Now write a passage with the title 'My Earliest Memories.'

Tip

Remember that in 'information' writing, descriptions, punctuation, grammar, spelling and presentation are just as important as they are in a story.

26 Writing an informal letter

Do you remember how to set out a letter? You may be offered a letter as an option in your SATs writing test, so refresh your memory now!

An informal letter to a friend can be 'chatty' in style and can contain punctuation such as exclamation marks which would not usually be included in more formal letters.

Do not feed the seals

121, Livingstone Road,
Smalborough.
SM1 3AB.
17th June

friendly tone of greeting

Dearest Shushi,

informal language

It was great to see you yesterday! We really must meet more often, talking on the phone just isn't quite the same, is it? I was wondering if you'd like to go out for the day soon — perhaps to the Sea Life Centre? I went last year, and the rescued seals were gorgeous! I'm sending a photo. I spent far too much money in the shop, because they had lots of great models of sea creatures, and some delicious fudge! Anyway, I'm sorry this is such a short note, but I must dash or I'll miss the post. Give my love to Prem and Jai. I'll give you a ring next week to arrange our outing.

Love, ▷ *friendly, informal goodbye*
Lynn ▷ *informal use of first name*

Activity

Write a letter to a friend or relative using an informal style.

Tip

Make sure your letter is well organised, and contains enough detail to be interesting to the reader.

27 Writing a formal letter

Look at this formal letter of complaint.

3A, Maple Street,
Charlottesville,
Leaming.
LT2 1CB.

17.1.99

formal tone of greeting

Dear Sir/Madam, *formal language*

I am writing to complain about a computer game 'Swamp Rats From Mars 3' I purchased on 12th September (receipt enclosed). I tried to load the game, and nothing happened; all I saw was a blank screen. When I took it back to my local branch of 'Computer Citadel' to make an exchange, your staff were rather unhelpful. They suggested I had damaged the game myself whilst loading it. The manageress refused to exchange the game and when I complained she suggested that I write to you at Head Office for an explanation of company policy on refunds. I shall expect to hear from you shortly with an explanation and a refund of the £35.99 I spent on the game. *formal language (informal: I'd)*

Yours faithfully, *formal 'goodbye'*

A. Zander *formal use of name – title (Mr), initial and surname*

Mr A Zander

Activity

Ask your parents or another adult in your family if they have a formal letter they do not mind you reading. Compare it with the informal letter on page 32, or one you have written yourself.

Tip

If you write a letter in your SATs test, you must write in the correct style for the kind of letter you have chosen to write.

28 Test 2

1. Write a formal letter of complaint to a theme park that did not live up to your expectations – it was dirty, the facilities were poor and some of the attractions were closed. Compare your letter with the example on page 33.

2. Write a chatty, informal letter to a friend you met on holiday. What have you done since you got back? Compare your letter with the example on page 32.

3. Write a story. Choose one of these story titles. Remember to plan before you write and to check your plan against the checklist on page 27.

- Whispers
- The Red Moon of Caldron 3
- The Darkened Room
- The Touch of Silver
- Wildlife Encounter!
- Island of Tomorrow

4. Write an article for your class newspaper about your hobby.

Formal letter checklist

- address: correctly set out?
- formal greeting: Dear Sir/Madam – or the name of the person you are writing to, if you know it.
- formal language: no chatty sentences or slang words such as 'OK'.
- correct farewell: 'Yours faithfully'.
- your full formal title and name: Mr, Miss or Ms and your initial, plus your last name.

Informal letter checklist

- address: correctly set out.
- greeting: friendly and personal, your friend's first name.
- informal language: you can use a chatty style and include slang terms, exclamation marks and question marks.
- friendly farewell: can be 'love', 'best wishes', 'see you soon' or something similar.
- the name your friend calls you: your first name, or even a nickname.

29 Speech marks

Do you know where to put speech marks when you are writing a story? Look at the example below.

'What's the matter?' Sophie whispered.

'I can hear an awful noise,' he said.

'Like what exactly? I can't hear anything,' Sophie muttered.

'Like a huge, scaly monster,' he said. 'And it's close by!'

'There are no such things as monsters,' said Sophie, sounding much more confident than she felt.

'It's getting closer!' squealed Henry, near to tears.

'Don't be silly,' Sophie hissed. 'This is the middle of London, not some swamp or haunted moor like in those ridiculous books you read.'

'That's no guarantee of safety,' whined Henry. 'Look what Reptillar did to Tokyo in *Night of the Radioactive Lizardmen!*'

'Look at this!' exclaimed Sophie, as she pounced on the source of the snorting, which had been hiding in the shrubbery.

'It's just a hedgehog,' sighed Henry with relief.

Sometimes words can give you a clue about where you should put speech marks. There are many different words to show a person has spoken, not just 'said'! Here are some:

commented, remarked, announced, spoke, uttered, interrupted, replied, responded

Some 'said' words tell you the way in which someone spoke:

cried, shouted, shrieked, screamed, yelled, bawled, grumbled, hollered

Many 'said' words describe the sound that someone made when speaking:

groaned, gurgled, murmured, mumbled

Animal sounds can describe people's speech:

bellowed, growled, roared, bleated, squeaked

Question

Underline all the words in the passage that mean 'said'.

Tip

Make sure you know when to use full stops, capital letters, commas, exclamation and question marks and speech marks.

30 Apostrophes

An apostrophe can be used to show that something belongs to someone. When used in this way, it is called a 'possessive apostrophe'. There are rules to help us to use possessive apostrophes correctly.

If it is a single noun doing the possessing (Judith, cat) the apostrophe comes after the noun and is followed by an **s**.

> It is Judith**'s** bag.
> The cat**'s** tail was very fluffy.
> This is Lindsey**'s** hat.
> Rafik**'s** hat is stripey.
> That plate is Daniel**'s**.

If it is a plural noun that does the possessing, the apostrophe still comes after the noun. If the noun already ends in **s**, no extra **s** is added. If the noun does not already end in **s**, an **s** is added after the apostrophe.

> The children**'s** gloves are smaller than the adults**'** gloves.
> The dogs**'** bowls are both empty.
> The babies**'** bottles are full of milk.

An apostrophe can also show us where a letter is missing. This happens where two words are joined.

e.g.   did not   didn't   is not   isn't
        cannot   can't   I have   I've

Be careful about **its** and **it's**.
- When **its** is used to show possession, there is no apostrophe: 'Give the cat **its** milk.'
- When **it's** is short for **it is** is there is an apostrophe: '**It's** a shame that **it's** raining.'

Question

Write down the short forms of these phrases:

they are

could not

will not

Tip

Plural nouns are the most difficult to make possessive.

Remember: if the noun ends in **s**, just add an apostrophe.

If the noun does not end in **s**, add an apostrophe and an **s**.

Test 3

1. Write out the following passage on paper putting in speech marks where they are needed. Remember to use a new line for each new speaker!

Not again, Alex sighed as he saw the broken vase on the floor. It wasn't me, said Bethany. I saw one of the cats disappearing at speed out of the back door as I came in. Which cat? asked Alex. That one! shouted Bethany, as a small black cat shot past, dodging between them. There was a crash from the living room. Oh no! There he goes again! said Alex.

2. Write out these sentences on paper, putting the possessive apostrophe in the correct place.

1. That dogs blanket needs washing.
2. The policemens buttons are shiny.
3. Those are Lauras sweets
4. The childrens tickets cost £1.50.
5. Beths hair is beautiful.
6. The bats communal roost is in that cave.

3. Write the shortened words for:

cannot _____	you have _____	I have _____
would not _____	they are _____	I would _____
should not _____	you are _____	she has _____
has not _____	he has _____	we have _____

32 Improving your spelling

Are there any words you often spell incorrectly?
Learn your words using Look, Cover, Write, Check.

1 **Look** at the word to try to memorise the pattern. Look at the shape of the word; are there any 'sticks' (as in b, d) or any 'tails' (as in p, q)?

2 **Cover** the word. Try to keep a picture of it in your 'mind's eye'.

3 **Write** the word down. Many adults do this to check whether a spelling 'looks right'.

4 **Check** the word. Have you spelled it correctly? If not, give yourself a tick under the correct letters, and try again concentrating on the letters that are wrong.

Question

Read the definition, look at the letters, rearrange them and write the word.

on purpose:
l e d e a t b i r e

odd, strange:
l e p c i r a u

Tip

Say the words you are trying to learn normally, then try to break them down into 'chunks' of sound:
caterpillar
cat – er – pill – ar
alligator
all – ig – at – or

Activity

Look at your language book at school and make a note of words you find difficult.

33 Some spelling 'rules'

Making plurals (words for 'more than one')

Sometimes words change their spelling when they are made plural. Some keep the same spelling and add an **s**. Some words stay exactly the same! How do you know which is which? These rules will help you.

Many words simply add an **s** :
cat   cat**s**   coat   coat**s**

Words that end in **s** add **es** :
bus   bus**es**

Words that end in **ch** or **sh** add **es** :
brush   brush**es**   ranch   ranch**es**

Words that end in **x** or **z** add **es** :
box   box**es**

Most words that end in **f** or **fe** change to **ve + s**
dwarf   dwar**ves**   wife   wi**ves**

CAUTION: there are some tricky exceptions to this rule:
roofs, chiefs, beliefs

Some really strange words stay the same: deer, sheep

Some seem to follow no pattern and just need learning:
man   men
woman   women
mouse   mice (tricky, because 'house' does not become 'hice'!)

Question

What are the plurals of these words?

fox

handkerchief

aircraft

glass

pot

Activity

Find more examples of words which end in s, ch, sh, x, f, fe. Now write the plurals for these words. Check your answers in a dictionary.

34 Ideas to help you with spelling

Look for 'words within words'

interest **has two:** in **and** rest
something **has two:** some **and** thing
comfortable **has two:** for **and** table

Memorising the shorter words will help you to remember longer ones.

Kit
Kite

Say spellings 'out loud'

This can help you with unexpected, difficult spellings, such as 'silent' or 'hidden' letters:

cupboard **said as** cup board helps you to remember the silent **p.**

Remember silent **e** changes the sound of a vowel in a word:

mop **becomes** mope, kit **becomes** kite.

Look for common patterns

- **letters which are grouped together** to make sounds:
  ight as in fight, might, height
- **common consonant blends** and the way in which particular consonants blend to make a sound:
  br, ch, ck, tr, pl, etc.
- **common vowel blends** and how two vowels blend together to make a particular sound:
  ou as in mouth, south; oi as in foil, boil;
  oa as in coat, boat.

Question

To which of these words can you add a silent **e** to make a new word? Write the words.

plan
grim
secret
man
lid
ton

Activity

Look back at the passage on page 4. Find 'words within words'. Make a list of other words which have words within them.

Tip

When you are trying to learn spellings, focus on a short list for 5 minutes each day.

35 Spelling games

Word Chain Game

You use the last letter of the previous word to make the next word.

newspape**r** – **r**ingin**g** – **g**allo**p** – **p**rincipl**e** –
elephan**t** – **t**antru**m** – **m**ello**w** – **w**hic**h** –
har**p** – **p**ea**r** – **r**ipe

Now it's your turn! Write down the words as you think of them, and check your spelling with a dictionary. Learn new spellings with the 'Look, Cover, Write, Check' system (see page 38).

See how long you can make your chain. Why not challenge your friends to a competition to see who can make the longest chain?

All Change!

This game will help you to learn a collection of spellings – and have fun at the same time! Write down a word. The next word in the chain can begin with any letter of the previous word, but here's the tricky part – it must use all of the following letters in that word!

Here is an example:

part**ner** – **ner**vo**us** – **us**ual – **al**liga**tor** – **tor**rent
– **ent**ertain – **tain**ted – **ed**itor – **or**nament

Some letter strings occur at the end of words, but never at the beginning. Look at these endings: nk, ng, nt.

Question

Can you think of more letter strings that only occur at the ends of words?

Activity

Start an **All Change!** word chain beginning: ti**me** me**tal** **al** ...

Tip

When you play word games, make sure you check new spellings with a dictionary before you learn them!

36 Common mistakes

Homophones are words that sound the same, but have a different spelling and meaning. Mistakes are commonly made with: **to**, **too** and **two** and **there**, **their** and **they're**.

to
- is used with a destination: *We're going to school.*
- it is also used with a verb (doing word): *I want to eat my ice cream.*

too
- is used to mean 'as well': *Can I come too?*
- it is also used with adjectives (describing words): *It's too cold to go out.*
- and with quantity words: *Don't eat too many sweets or too much chocolate.*

two
- is the number *2*: *I have two hamsters and a rabbit.*

there
- is used to mean a place: *Look over there!*
- it is also used with **is**, **are**, **was** and **were**: *There is a factory where once there were green fields.*

their
- shows possession by more than one person or thing: *The kittens were chasing their tails.*

they're
- is the shortened form of **they are**: *They're playing in the garden.*

I see the sea!

Question

Cross out the wrong words in these sentences.

1 When I went to the cinema, my sister came **to too two**.
2 Who's **their they're there**?
3 Make sure you keep **to two too** of those cakes for me!
4 It's **too to two** hot today.
5 You need **too to two** be careful when you are using a sharp knife.
6 There are **to too two** many people on this beach!
7 **There their they're** are twelve tomatoes on my plant.
8 The children fetched **there their they're** coats.

Activity

Find other homophones such as these:

sail	sale
plane	plain
rain	reign
beach	beech

37 Test 4

Ask an adult to read these instructions and the passage below.

Instructions

Read out this passage to the child, who should write nothing while you are reading the first time. Read it again slowly. When you come to a word in blue, tell the child to write it down. This is similar to the spelling test administered by teachers during the SATs test.

Susan walked down the road towards the shops. She had been saving for weeks to buy the computer game, *Bugs 2 – The Challenge*. It was a beautiful frosty autumn morning. Susan was cold, but she barely seemed to notice. Her excitement carried her along, through the bustle of Saturday morning shoppers. Still, she rubbed her hands as she walked, then put them in her pockets. At that very moment, as she turned the corner into the High Street, she slipped on a patch of ice, and fell. Luck was not on Susan's side that day. As she lay sprawled on the pavement, she heard the last voice she wanted to hear, saying her name. She looked up to see the tallest, most handsome boy looking down at her. It was David, from school. He stretched his hand out to her to help her up. Susan imagined herself creeping away, like a bug from her game. She could almost hear the laughter of her friends as it echoed in her imagination. Susan uncoiled her legs, and tried to stand up casually. Unfortunately, as she brought her hand out of her pocket, pieces of old sweet wrapper fluttered to the ground, disturbed by her nervous fingers. David's shoulders shook. He tried to disguise a giggle as a sneeze. Susan looked at him in horrified silence. She remained on the floor for some time, not knowing what to do. David finally grasped her hand and pulled her to her feet, saying. "I'm just on my way to 'Computer World'. Do you want to come?" Susan smiled.

Count up the number of spellings you get right.

Below 10 You need to spend some time practising the spelling suggestions on pages 38–41. Try to learn a small group of new spellings every night. You will soon improve!

11 to 15 With a little practice, your spelling will be even better! Look again at the suggestions on pages 38–41, and keep a small notebook to learn new words as you find them.

16 to 20 Your spelling is good. To improve it even further, keep a small notebook to collect new words. You can even set yourself a target of finding and learning to spell ten new words a week. Imagine how wonderful your work will become!

 38 Letter formation and style

Make sure you are sitting in a comfortable position before you start to write. Make sure you are holding your pen correctly with your index finger and thumb, resting the shaft of the pen on your third finger.

Correct basic letter formation:

a b c d e f g h i j
k l m n o p q r s t
u v w x y z

⟶ = where it begins

Look at this piece of handwriting:

> My name is Jai. I am eleven years old. I like writing adventure stories and funny poems. When I am at home, I like to ride my bike and listen to music.

Jai's handwriting would earn her high marks in the handwriting test. Her writing flows together well, her joins are correct and her spacing is regular. Her letters are consistently sized. Capital letters, ascenders ('sticks' as on 'd'), and descenders ('tails' as on 'p') are the correct size.

Handwriting checklist

1 Is your handwriting easy to read?
2 Are the letters formed correctly?
3 Is the spacing between the letters regular?
4 Are the joins neat and regular?

39 Test 5

Choose a passage from the story you wrote for the exercise on page 28. Copy it onto paper in your very best handwriting.

When you have finished, look at the statements below, and see which one most closely matches your own writing. Be honest! Ask your mum or dad to check your writing against the statements too.

Tip

Remember that if you take care over the way in which you present your work, people will notice. The best work in the world is useless if no one can read it!

These statements are very similar to those used by the examiner during the SATs test, and the quality of the handwriting they refer to improves as you read down the list.

Statements

A My handwriting is easy to read, but the letters can be different sizes, and are not always the right shape. The spaces between my words and letters are not always the same.

B The shapes of my letters are usually correct. My upper and lower case letters (capitals are 'upper case' letters) are usually the correct size in relation to one another. Most of the spaces between my words and letters are correct

C My letters are always the correct size and shape. The spaces between my words and letters are correct. My handwriting is usually correctly joined.

D My handwriting is joined and flows well. The spaces between my words and letters are correct. My ascenders (the 'stick' on a d for example) and descenders (the 'tail' on a p for example) are consistently the correct size.

40 Be the editor!

In this book you have practised reading, writing, spelling, punctuation and handwriting. When you write for your SATs use **all** the skills you have learned.

An exciting story will be even better with careful spelling, punctuation and clear handwriting, so – be your own editor! **Always** read your work back to yourself. Make corrections as you go through it.

Use this checklist when 'editing' what you have written. If you practise reading and correcting your own work, it will be easy for you on the day of your SATs test!

1 Sentences
Have you used a new sentence for each thought or happening?

2 Paragraphs
Have you divided your work into paragraphs?
Does each paragraph show where a new idea begins?

3 Punctuation
Have you checked your punctuation?

- full stops
- commas
- apostrophes
- exclamation marks
- capital letters
- speech marks
- question marks

4 Spelling
Have you checked your spelling? Put a wiggly line in pencil under any words that don't look right. You can come back to them at the end of the test when you have finished the paper.

Tip

When you are reading, look at the way punctuation is used. Look out for different types of punctuation such as colons (:) and semi colons (;) and see if you can start to use them accurately in your own writing.

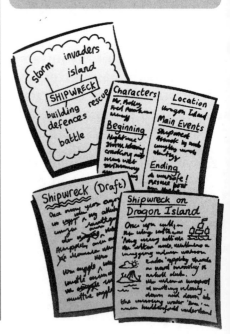

41 Extension to Level 6

Notes for parents

Children are only entered for the Level 6 Extension Paper if they have been consistently working at a 'high Level 5' throughout their time in Year 6. The Level 6 paper requires a sophisticated level of expression and understanding that exceeds the capabilities of most children in Year 6. Don't forget that a child in Year 6 is expected to attain Level 4, and has already exceeded targets for the age group by attaining Level 5!

If you find your child has been entered for the Level 6 paper, ask the school to provide you with some past papers to examine and perhaps practice at home. You will probably be surprised by the level of difficulty.

Provided below is a description of assessment criteria for Level 6. It closely reflects the criteria applied by SATs examiners.

> The piece of writing uses all the correct conventions of the relevant form (i.e. letter, information writing, etc.). Main issues all receive good coverage, and a wide range of information given in the text is concisely summarised. The piece shows a sustained awareness of the reader; there is a strong introduction, and an appropriate summary in the final paragraph. The reader's interest is sustained via a variety of devices such as appropriate detail and varied vocabulary. Ideas are appropriately organised into paragraphs, and the sequencing of the piece is consistent. A range of sentence structures is used to create effects, for example, a varied use of adjectives and adverbs giving shades of meaning, and devices such as alliteration may be used. Spelling is generally accurate, including irregular words. Presentation is good; the handwriting shows confidence and clarity.

Use the suggestions in the next column to help your child to work at the standard required to achieve Level 6.

Suggestions

• Read a variety of formats and genres – newspapers, magazine articles, collections of letters, etc. Discuss the differing styles and levels of formality with your child.

• Discuss the books your child reads with reference to characterisation, the devices that create mood and pace in writing, such as vocabulary, alliteration, onomatopoeia, etc., to which your child should be able to refer using the correct terminology.

• Look at poetry together and analyse how literary effects are created. Many study aids are available to guide you.

• Above all, be relaxed about the process of preparation. Your child may well feel under pressure to 'perform' in the SATs, but do not allow any sense of failure if Level 6 is not achieved. Point out that even being entered for the paper shows that the school holds your child's work in the highest regard.

GLOSSARY

adjective
a word used to describe a noun

alliteration
(Page 5) several words in a sentence with the same letter or sound

apostrophe
(Page 36) a punctuation mark that shows possession or omission

author
the person who wrote the book

bibliography
a list of books used by the author for research when writing a book

character
(Page 7) a person in a story

contents
(Page 1) a list of the main topics covered in a non-fiction book, usually at the beginning

dust cover
a protective paper cover found on many hardback books

fiction
(Page 17) 'made up' books – story books

glossary
a list of useful words and their meanings

homophone
(Page 42) a word which sounds the same as another word but has a different meaning

illustrator
the person who drew the pictures

index
an alphabetical list of subjects mentioned in a non-fiction book, usually at the end

ISBN
International Standard Book Number: every book has its own identifying number

motive
(Page 14) the reason someone has for doing something

non-fiction
(Page 17) factual books; information books

onomatopoeia
(Page 5) words that sound like the thing they describe

pen portrait
a short piece of writing about the author

phrase
a small group of words that make sense

plot
what happens in a story

profile
(Page 8) an outline; a brief description

publisher's logo
a picture or graphic used by a publisher: Puffin books have a puffin

quotation
a phrase or sentence copied exactly from a text, shown in inverted commas

scanning
(Page 20) looking for key words or phrases in a text to find the information you need

skimming
(Page 20) reading through a passage quickly to find out what it is about

synopsis
a short piece of writing that summarises the main events in a story

thesaurus
(Pages 6, 26) a book containing words and lists of words with the same meaning

verb
a word expressing an action, often called a 'doing word'